This book is dedicated to:

_____
(Name of Child)

May you take a trip that is the adventure of your life.

Copyright © 2023 by Dr. Pamela Gurley

All Rights Reserved.

No part of this publication may be reproduced, distributed, or transmitted in any form or by any means, including photocopying, recording, or other electronic or mechanical methods, without the prior written permission of the publisher, except in the case of brief quotations embodied in a book review and certain other noncommercial uses permitted by copyright law.

For permission requests, send an email to: admin@clarkandhillenterprise.com

First Printing

Illustration by Amina Yaqoob

ISBN Hardcover: ISBN: 979-8-9858658-8-2

Printed in the United States of America

Clark and Hill Enterprise, LLC
6655 Santa Barbara Rd, #8681
Elkridge, MD 21075

www.clarkandhillenterprise.com
www.iamdrpgurley.com

Brown Girl and Brown Boy
Africa Adventures

Brown Girl and Brown Boy were very happy to be going on a trip to South Africa with their mom and dad for summer vacation.

They had always wanted to visit Johannesburg, and now they finally would get the chance to!

They both jumped with joy and excitement when they learned they were going.

They quickly packed their bags with clothes, books, games—everything they could need for the trip.

On the plane ride there, they giggled together while playing card games and looking out the window at all the fascinating sights below them.

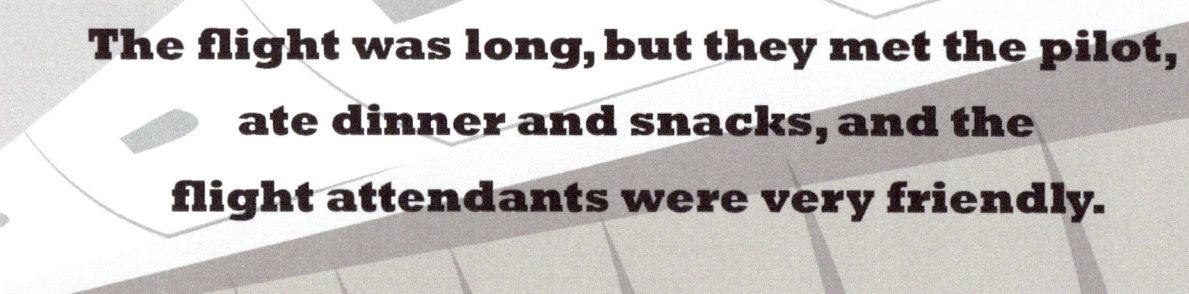

The flight was long, but they met the pilot, ate dinner and snacks, and the flight attendants were very friendly.

They finally arrived in the late afternoon,
and the airport was very busy,
and many people were waiting to be picked up.

They were met by their tour guide,
who drove them through the town,
pointing out some historic sites
on the way to the hotel.

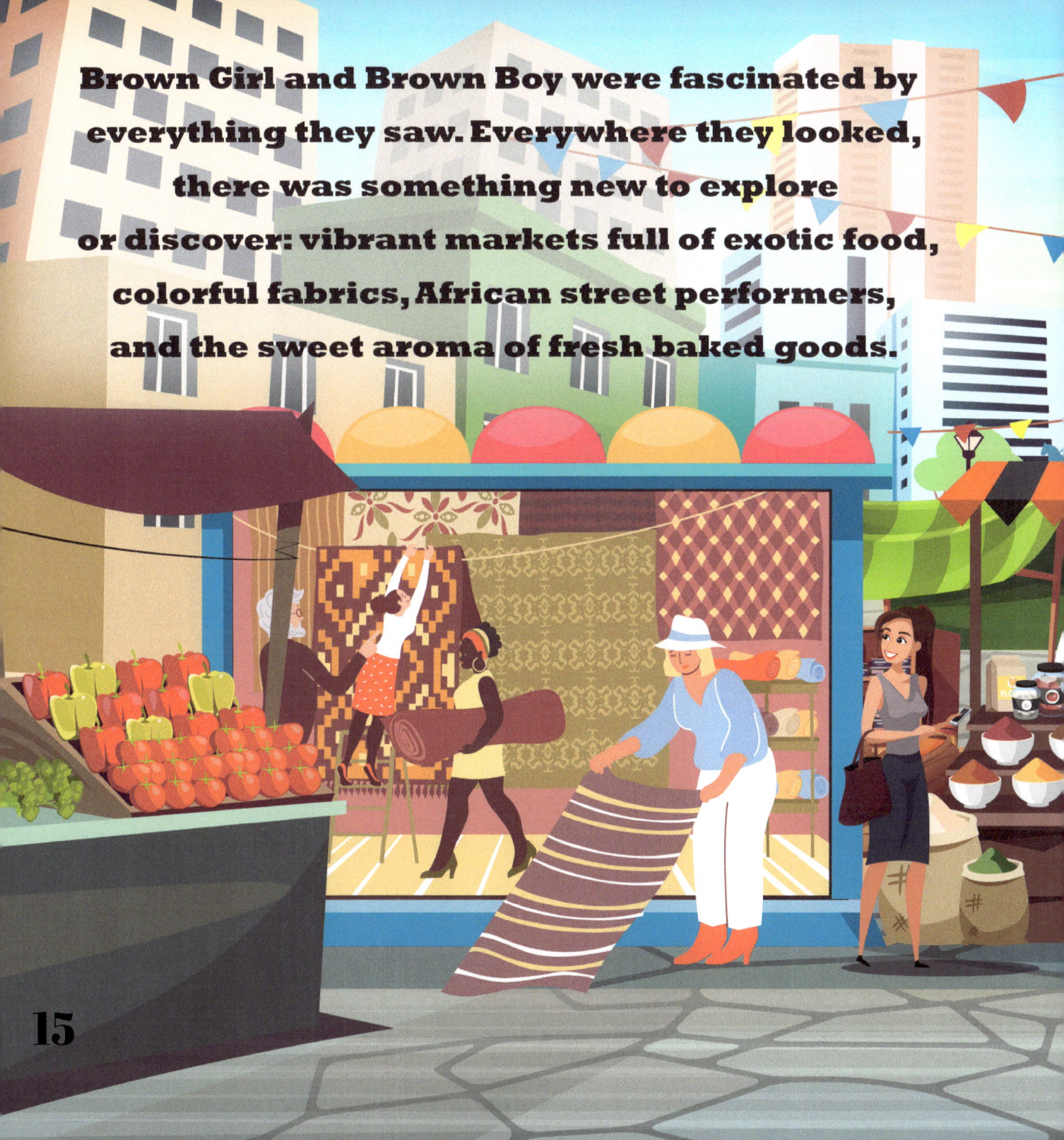

Brown Girl and Brown Boy were fascinated by everything they saw. Everywhere they looked, there was something new to explore or discover: vibrant markets full of exotic food, colorful fabrics, African street performers, and the sweet aroma of fresh baked goods.

They finally got to the hotel, which was fancy, like the ones in the United States. There were lots of mirrors on the walls and accented with black and red furniture.

Brown Girl and Brown Boy had been
looking forward to this trip,
dreaming of the sights they would see,
the animals they would observe,
and the culture they would experience.

But despite their enthusiasm,
both were exhausted
from the time difference!

Their parents tucked them into bed early that evening, promising an exciting day ahead. Little did they know what was waiting for them on this trip!

The next morning, Brown Girl and Brown Boy woke up very early to eat breakfast. As soon as breakfast was finished (which included some delicious South African specialties!), everyone packed some snacks and headed out for the day.

The first stop of the day was Lion Park - a refuge where lions roam free within a large fenced-in area. "We get to see animals like lions!" yelled Brown Boy as he jumped up and down excitedly.

It was breathtakingly beautiful!
Not only could you observe these lions up close,
but you could also feed them right from your
hand - something which made Brown Girl's eyes
light up with delight!

After spending the morning at Lion Park, Brown Girl and Brown Boy were off to another adventure – a Safari.

Brown Girl and Brown Boy couldn't wait to see all the animals up close - lions, elephants, giraffes - oh my! As soon as they got in the jeep with their parents and the guide, they spotted animals roaming everywhere.

They spotted a monkey in the tree, elephants, and buffalo. They even saw sleeping lions, giraffes eating from tall trees, and zebra. They were excited, pointing at every animal they saw.

Brown Girl and Brown Boy quickly grabbed binoculars to get a closer look at all the animals around them - hippos lounging in ponds, giraffes reaching up high for leaves off trees, zebras running across the plains - wow!

They continued through the safari until evening came along, and it was time for dinner back at the hotel.

Brown Girl and Brown Boy shared stories from what they had seen throughout the day while eating the traditional African cuisine Pap en vleis, which is a corn porridge and meat. It was delicious!

Then it was bedtime so that everyone could rest up for another amazing day exploring South Africa again.

The family visited museums where they learned about South African culture and history; swam with dolphins at Seal Island; explored caves filled with ancient fossils; hiked up mountains covered in lush vegetation…the list went on and on!

One of their favorites was visiting a wildlife education campsite where kids could learn about conservation efforts through interactive activities.

Two weeks had passed by quickly.
The days just flew by because there was
always something fun to do.
Every night they would come back from
their adventures exhausted but with
huge smiles on their faces.

After exploring other parts of South Africa over the next few days, including taking a tour to Soweto and around Table Mountain, it was time for their adventurers abroad to come to an end.

Brpwn Girl and Brown Boy loved
every second of their trip -
it was an incredible experience
that will stay with them forever.

As much fun as it would have been to stay longer, they had what felt like a lifetime of exciting adventures - there really was no place quite like it anywhere else in the world!

Brown Girl and Brown Boy boarded the plane with their mom and dad, with loads of wonderful stories about their time in Johannesburg tucked away inside their hearts.

Safe Travels!

About the Author

Dr. Pamela Gurley is a Content Strategy Expert, International Speaker, and World-Renowned Best-Selling Author, and Media Journalist who understands the power of words (both verbal and written). As the Founder/CEO of Clark and Hill Enterprise and IAMDRPGURLEY and Founder/President of the Brown Girl and Brown Boy Literacy Foundation, she is on a mission to empower, grow, transform, and motivate others, as well as lead and challenge social norms and false narratives.

Dr. Gurley's 26-year career includes working as a civil servant for 14 years for the United States Federal Government across the Bureau of Alcohol, Tobacco, Firearms, and Explosives, Department of the Army, Department of Defense, Department of State, and the Merit Systems Protection Board. Dr. Gurley's budget, management, and leadership experience extend domestically and internationally across several continents and countries. She resigned from her federal career as a GS-15 to become a full-time entrepreneur on November 7, 2020. In November 2019, Dr. Gurley released her first book, "I Am Not A Stereotype: I Am H.E.R.," and it lit a different path in her love of writing. In March 2021, she released her second book, Bl@ck Girl Activist, becoming an Amazon Best Seller; and on June 3, 2021, she released the first three sets of books in her Brown Girl and Brown Boy multilingual children's books series. She has since published five additional titles totaling 21 books. She has also been a part of three anthologies – one with Dr. Gurley as a Visionary Author. She is a retired United States Army Veteran and holds a Bachelor of Arts in Psychology, a Master's in Health Service Administration, and a Doctorate in Management with a concentration in Organizational Development and Change.

Other Books by the Author:

English:
- Brown Boy Be Social
- Brown Girl, Be Social
- Brown Boy, Break Barriers
- Brown Boy, Break Barriers
- Brown Girl, and Brown Boy, Be Well
- Brown Girl, and Brown Boy, Be Mindful
- Brown Girl and Brown Boy, We Love Hobbies

Spanish:
- Niña Morena, Sé Sociable
- Niño Moreno, Sé Sociable
- Niña Morena, Rompe Barreras
- Niño Moreno, Rompe Barreras
- Niña Morena y Niño Moreno, Manténganse Saludables
- Niña Morena y Niño Moreno, Sean Considerables
- Niña morena y niño moreno, Nos (encantan) los pasatiempos

French:
- Petite Fille Noire, Sois Sociable
- Petit Garçon Noir, Sois Sociable
- Petit Garçon Noir, Brises Barrières
- Petite Fille Noire, Brises Barrières
- Petite Fille Noire et Petit Garçon Noir, Allez Bien
- Petite Fille Noire et Petit Garçon Noir, Soyez Prévenants
- Petite Fille Noire et Petit Garçon Noir, Nous Vivons des Loisirs

www.ingramcontent.com/pod-product-compliance
Lightning Source LLC
Chambersburg PA
CBHW040723060526

44119CB00083B/302